#Don't TagMe

J.L. Sterling, B.Ed

Title: *#Don't Tag Me: Why Sharenting Could Be the Biggest Parenting Mistake of the Digital Age*
Author: J.L. Sterling, B.Ed
First Edition: 2025
ISBN: 978-1-7638935-4-2
Cover design and interior layout by Aussie Guy's Books
This is a work of nonfiction. Names and identifying details may have been changed to protect individual privacy.

#Don'tTagMe

Don't Tag Me

Why 'Sharenting' Could Be the Biggest Parenting Mistake of the Digital Age!

Don'tTagMe

Reader's Guide

This book is written with deep care for both parents and children. Some sections will feel emotionally confronting, while others will feel practical or reassuring. The tone shifts intentionally throughout~each part designed to evoke reflection, clarity, and compassion. Below is a guide to the emotional tone of each section, so you can move through the book with awareness and self-kindness.

Part I: The Digital Childhood We Never Lived

These chapters offer insight into how digital culture evolved faster than parenting norms could keep up. This is not a critique~it's an invitation to rethink.

Part II: Through Their Eyes: The Child's Perspective

These pages may feel personal. They give voice to children who have been unintentionally exposed, misrepresented, or hurt by the online visibility imposed on them.

Part III: Behind the Camera: The Parent's Dilemma

These chapters unpack why parents share and how we can recalibrate our habits~without guilt, just awareness and gentle accountability.

Part IV: The Research We Can't Ignore

A credible, grounded look at empirical studies. This section supports what many of us already suspect with hard data and professional analysis.

Part V: The Consequences No One Talks About

These chapters contain some of the most confronting stories~bullying, trauma, even suicide. Read with care. Their inclusion is purposeful, not sensational.

Part VI: Protecting the Next Generation

This part is full of tools, boundaries, and checklists. The tone is encouraging~because change is always possible.

Part VII: Legacy & Leadership

These final reflections are about the future. They offer a compassionate and aspirational path forward for parents, carers, and educators alike.

Preface

For more than three decades, I have stood in classrooms and community spaces, observing the ways children grow, learn, and connect. As a parent of three and a teacher of thousands, I have seen firsthand the power of visibility ~ and its shadow side.

When I began using Facebook in 2008, my posts mirrored those of so many other parents. My family was active, constantly outdoors, involved in sport and travel. I posted wins, scenery, milestones, and our pets doing silly things. It was a digital scrapbook ~ innocent, even joyful.

But digital habits evolve quietly. What started as memory-keeping began to look more like performance. Over time, the camera turned outward ~ then inward. The subjects were no longer landscapes or trophies ~ they were our children.

We didn't see it happening. Most of us didn't mean for it to happen. But it did.

This book is not written from a place of judgment. It comes from lived experience, painful reflection, and the stories I have gathered over a lifetime of teaching.

The story that left the deepest imprint was that of Amanda Todd ~ a Canadian teenager who died by suicide in 2012 after being harassed and shamed online. Before she died, she posted a video using flashcards to tell her story. One of them read:

"I'm struggling to stay in this world, because everything just touches me so deeply... I'm doing this to be an inspiration and to

9

show that I can be strong... Everyone has a story, and everyone's future will be bright one day, you just gotta pull through. I'm still here aren't I?"

Her words echo in every hallway I walk, every quiet student I teach. Her video was titled *"My Story: Struggling, Bullying, Suicide, Self Harm."*

We must do better.

Language shapes understanding. In linguistics, a *portmanteau* is a word formed by blending two existing ones, combining both sound and meaning. Examples include *smog* (smoke + fog) and *motel* (motor + hotel). *Sharenting* is a portmanteau too ~ formed from *sharing* and *parenting*.

This book invites you to unpack this word with me ~ and everything it has come to represent.

It is not a textbook, though it includes research. It is not a lecture, though it makes a case. It is an invitation. To pause. To reconsider. To protect what we love most, before we post.

I want parents to feel empowered, not ashamed. I want children to be protected, not displayed. And I want our communities to be honest, informed, and supportive.

This is not a how-to guide. It is a why-we-must guide.

Welcome to *Don't Tag Me*.

#Don'tTagMe

Contents

Introduction 17

Part I: The Digital Childhood We Never Lived............................ 19

When Posting Became Parenting 21

The Rise of the Child Influencer 24

Devices Before Dialogue 27

The Myth of 'Nothing to Hide'... 30

Part II: Through Their Eyes ~ The Child's Perspective 33

The Silent Witnesses 35

Tagged Without a Voice... 37

When Trust Starts to Fracture 39

The Hidden Scars of Sharenting.. 41

**PART III: Public by Default ~ Privacy, Consent, & Digital
Boundaries 43**

When Consent Isn't a Click 45

Digital Imprints and Future Identity... 48

Platforms and Prompts 51

When the Digital Footprint Becomes a Shadow 54

PART IV: Behind the Screen ~ What & Why Parents Share........... 57

Memory, Meaning, and the Modern Scrapbook 59

Validation, Comparison, and the Performative Parent 61

The Business of the Baby Photo.. 64

The Platform's Pull ~ Designed to Keep You Sharing.................. 66

When Sharing Heals and When It Harms.................................... 68

13

Part V: The Why Behind the Post **71**

Memory, Meaning, and the Modern Scrapbook 73

Validation, Comparison, and the Performative Parent 76

When the Feed Becomes a File 80

Consent in the Age of the Algorithm 83

The Hidden Curriculum of Exposure 86

When the Law Lags Behind 89

The Long Memory of the Internet 93

Who Owns the Digital You? 96

The Algorithmic Parent 99

Part VI: Reclaiming Boundaries ~ How to Move Forward **103**

Pause Before You Post 105

Consent Starts at Home 109

The Moment They Say "Stop" 113

From Performative to Protective 117

Through Their Eyes ~ What Kids Wish We Knew 121

The Parent-Child Digital Agreement 125

What If We Get It Right? 129

PART VII: Legacy & Leadership **131**

What Will They Remember? 133

The "Don't Tag Me" Manifesto 136

Endnotes 139

Academic Resource Summaries 141

The Call to Action 143

#PauseBeforeYouPost 145

#Don'tTagMe

Introduction

Somewhere between the first baby photo we shared and the tenth birthday post we celebrated online, a new kind of parenting quietly emerged. We didn't name it at first. We were busy capturing milestones, sharing joy, and connecting with others.

Then the term arrived:
'Sharenting'

It didn't come with a manual. It didn't announce itself as a cultural shift. It slipped into our routines, wrapped in good intentions.

Sharing became so natural that we didn't stop to ask:
What story are we telling about our children?
Who is this really for?
And what might it cost them later?

This book is for every parent who's ever uploaded a photo with pride. For every teacher who's seen the aftermath in a student's eyes. For every child who has been digitally documented before they could even say the word "privacy."

We live in an era where children have digital identities before they have physical autonomy. They're tagged, tracked, and displayed in ways that many of us never imagined when we first became parents — or teachers.

In these pages, you'll find stories, research, questions, and guidance. But more than anything, you'll find space. Space to reflect. To reconsider. And to reclaim the parts of childhood that still deserve to be sacred.

We will not get this perfect. That's not the goal. The goal is to become more conscious.

If we can shift the conversation from *performance to protection*, from *exposure to respect*, from *instant sharing to intentional pause*, then we've already begun.

Let's begin.

Part I: The Digital Childhood We Never Lived

#Don'tTagMe

Chapter 1

When Posting Became Parenting

There was a time when parenting was something you did, not something you posted.

Before smartphones sat in every pocket and apps filled with filters and share buttons became second nature, the daily rhythm of parenting was lived quietly and personally. Moments of pride were shared in person ~ over the phone, through a handwritten note, or at a family gathering. Memories were tucked into photo albums and shoeboxes ~ not into cloud servers or Instagram feeds.

But something changed. And for many parents, that change arrived the day they made their first post.

For me, it was 2008. I joined Facebook like many others ~ curious, excited, and looking for connection. My children were young, active, and constantly surprising me with their talents, their humour, and their joy. As a family, we travelled, played sports, went on camping trips, and lived fully. Capturing these moments felt natural. Sharing them felt generous.

There was no ill intent. I wanted to document our lives. I wanted relatives to see the grand final goal, the silly face painted at a carnival, the moment we reached the summit of a long hike. At the time, it felt like a new way to love loudly.

But I now recognise that something else was unfolding beneath the surface ~ something cultural, something collective. What started as connection slowly morphed into performance.

As more parents joined the platforms, our feeds filled with curated childhoods. We began to measure milestones by engagement. The more we shared, the more it felt expected. Proud moments became polished content. Messy realities were cropped out. And parenting ~ at least the visible parts of it ~ began to live online.

It's important to pause here and ask ourselves why.

We shared out of love. Out of joy. Out of the deeply human desire to be seen and validated in our efforts. Parenting is hard. It is relentless, exhausting, and often invisible. Social media gave many of us a way to be witnessed ~ to feel like what we were doing mattered. That our kids were thriving. That we were doing it right.

But as our motivations shifted ~ from memory to community to performance ~ we stopped asking one crucial question:

Is this moment mine to share?

We were the first generation of parents to walk this path. There were no digital blueprints. No handbooks. Just apps, trends, and a slowly growing awareness that this new parenting landscape came with risks we hadn't imagined.

That's what this chapter invites ~ not guilt, but pause. Not shame, but insight. Parenting doesn't need to be perfect ~ it never has been. But as we navigate this digital terrain, we can begin to question what it means to parent in public, and whether visibility should ever come before protection.

We cannot rewind the clock, but we can rewrite the script. And we start by remembering that being a parent is not the same as being a poster.

Chapter 2

The Rise of the Child Influencer

In the early days of social media, children appeared in posts as joyful participants in family memories. But over time, something began to shift. The camera turned more frequently. The moments became more polished. And somewhere along the way, the child became the brand.

The rise of the child influencer wasn't a singular event. It was gradual, almost invisible. One post led to another. One viral clip led to a sponsorship. One birthday video turned into a following. Platforms like YouTube and Instagram didn't just host family content ~ they began to reward it.

And for some parents, it offered a new kind of opportunity.

Many of these families were not chasing fame. They were sharing joy, looking for community, or creating something they thought would benefit others. But social media rewards consistency, visibility, and engagement. Suddenly, children were no longer just in the frame ~ they were the content.

Outfits were coordinated. Reactions were filmed. Playtime became production time. A tantrum could be edited into a comedic reel. A milestone became a monetised post. Brands

24

began partnering with families to feature products. Followers began watching closely. And children, often without understanding, became influencers before they could spell their own name.

It's not that these parents didn't care. In most cases, they cared deeply. But the cultural current was moving quickly ~ and few paused to ask what it meant for the child.

For the child influencer, there are no auditions, no contracts, no agents. There is rarely consent. They are filmed, watched, and distributed ~ sometimes millions of times over. Their private lives become entertainment. Their most vulnerable or joyful moments are played back for strangers. And often, they do not know what they are giving away.

This isn't just about followers or fame. It's about the psychology of visibility.

What happens to a child who learns that attention equals love? That praise is measured in hearts and comments? That their value is tied to how well they perform their own life? What do they do when they no longer want to be filmed, or when adolescence arrives and their digital childhood follows them into high school?

There is a growing number of teenagers now speaking out ~ children of influencers who grew up online. Some feel betrayed. Others feel confused by the digital legacy they didn't choose. Many feel like their identity was shaped without them. And some are taking legal action to reclaim their image, their name, or their narrative.

Even for families who never went viral, the influencer culture has had an impact. Everyday parents now feel pressure to "capture content" rather than simply live moments. And everyday children now live under the quiet tension of being watched.

This chapter isn't about criticism. It's about caution. We can celebrate our children without centering them as content. We can share moments without turning them into stories we monetize. We can be proud ~ and private.

Because every child deserves the chance to grow up without being someone else's feed.

Chapter 3

Devices Before Dialogue

The first time a child holds a tablet, swipes a screen, or taps an icon, a doorway opens ~ not just to entertainment, but to influence.

In many homes, devices have become the default companion of childhood. They soothe, distract, occupy. They're present at the dinner table, in the back seat, at family gatherings. A restless toddler? Hand them a phone. A bored teenager? Let them scroll. Devices are woven into the fabric of daily life ~ often with more intimacy than conversation.

But when devices come before dialogue, something subtle shifts in the family dynamic. Screens begin to speak more loudly than stories passed across the table. Eye contact is replaced by algorithms. The rhythm of relational trust is interrupted by the tap of a notification.

We are not bad parents for giving our children devices. We are overwhelmed parents, tired parents, well-intentioned parents living in an age of digital saturation. But when devices become the mediator between parent and child ~ or worse, the substitute for engagement ~ we must pause.

We are teaching children how to communicate, how to bond, how to feel safe. If they learn these things from apps instead of adults, they miss the layers of emotional wisdom that only human connection can offer.

What's more, the device becomes a two-way mirror. Children don't just consume. They begin to document. They point the lens at themselves. They learn to filter, crop, record, and perform. They mimic what they see ~ not just influencers, but their own parents. They start to curate their identity before they've even formed it.

Parents, too, are caught in this dynamic. It's easier to post a photo than have a hard conversation. It's easier to share a win than hold space for a meltdown. Digital connection becomes a stand-in for real intimacy ~ even with our own children.

But silence accumulates. So does absence.

Children don't always ask for presence in ways we recognize. They may not say "I need to talk," but they'll act out. Withdraw. Lash out. Scroll endlessly. Their behaviour becomes the dialogue we're missing. And devices, for all their design, cannot decode the emotional needs beneath that silence.

To reclaim our presence, we don't need to eliminate technology. We need to re-establish relationship. That starts with asking: What matters more ~ the moment itself or the way we package it?

Children remember the tone of our voice more than the caption. They remember the way we looked at them, not the way we framed the shot.

The conversations we have offline become the compass for how our children navigate life online. If we want to raise thoughtful, compassionate, emotionally grounded children, it starts not with screen time limits, but with our willingness to talk, listen, and be there ~ fully.

Devices are powerful. But they are tools ~ not teachers.

Let us return to dialogue.

Chapter 4

The Myth of 'Nothing to Hide'

It is often said with casual confidence: "If you have nothing to hide, you have nothing to fear."

But that sentiment unravels when we place it in the hands of a child.

Children are not born with a sense of privacy. They learn it ~ slowly, organically, through experience. They learn it when we knock before entering their room. When we ask before opening their journal. When we let them choose what to wear or how to speak about their feelings. Privacy is not about secrecy ~ it is about dignity.

And yet, online, we treat their stories differently. We post bath time pictures. We share medical updates. We caption their meltdowns. We broadcast their report cards. We joke about their quirks. We upload videos of their reactions, their tears, their triumphs.

Sometimes these posts are met with laughter or likes. But underneath them is a question that rarely gets asked:

What would this child say if they were older and saw this?

What story are we telling on their behalf?

The myth of "nothing to hide" implies that visibility is neutral ~ that if there is no wrongdoing, there is no harm. But for a child, the harm isn't about guilt. It's about exposure.

They are not hiding anything. They are simply not ready.

A toddler may not understand what it means to have their photo shared with thousands. A nine-year-old may not grasp that a funny clip could resurface in high school. A teenager may feel violated, even if the post seemed innocent.

And while the child might not articulate these feelings directly, they carry the weight of them. They begin to feel watched. Evaluated. Branded. Their sense of self becomes interwoven with an audience they never chose.

As parents, we must remember: it is not our story to tell alone.

We are stewards of their image, guardians of their growing sense of identity. We are not their publicists. We are not their biographers. We are the keepers of their unfolding privacy.

And it begins with restraint.

Before we post, we must pause. Not because we're hiding anything, but because we honour what hasn't yet emerged.

Because childhood is not content ~ it is becoming.

And becoming deserves privacy.

#Don'tTagMe

Part II: Through Their Eyes ~ The Child's Perspective

#Don'tTagMe

Chapter 5

The Silent Witnesses

They sit quietly at the dinner table while their photos circle the globe.

Their face, their moment, their tears or triumph ~ immortalized in a caption and shared with hundreds or thousands of strangers. They don't complain, not at first. They know that asking questions can make things worse. They don't want to seem ungrateful, or dramatic. After all, their parents are proud. Their parents are sharing.

But deep inside, many children are confused. They're not sure why something that felt private has become so public. A toddler who didn't yet understand what it meant to have a digital presence becomes a tween who is suddenly self-conscious about it. A teen who once smiled for every picture now winces when the phone is raised.

They begin to notice that some moments are no longer theirs alone. The first day of school, the dentist visit, a meltdown in a supermarket aisle ~ all posted online with well-meaning but often insensitive captions. "He's terrified of the dentist again!" "First day jitters ~ fingers crossed she doesn't cry this year!"

It's not abuse. But it is an erosion of dignity. A slow burn. A subtle breach of boundaries.

Children don't always speak up because they don't yet have the language to describe what feels wrong. They might not understand digital privacy, but they know what embarrassment feels like. They might not grasp online permanence, but they understand when a classmate laughs at a post they never knew existed. They know the sting of a joke made at their expense. And they know the quiet ache of not being asked.

As a teacher, I've watched students withdraw emotionally when their parents post photos that should have stayed in the family. I've seen students huddle together at lunch, reacting in real time to content that was meant to showcase them but ended up exposing them. I've watched a child's enthusiasm fade because they feared what might be shared next.

And I've listened to students ~ children as young as eight ~ say things like, "I wish my mum would just ask me first." That single sentence says everything. They don't want a ban. They want a boundary. They want the courtesy of inclusion.

The silent witnesses are everywhere. They are not angry yet. But they are watching. And they are learning that their lives are not entirely their own.

They are learning that some of their most sacred memories have already been turned into content. And that trust ~ that deeply human need to feel safe in our own story ~ is more fragile than they knew.

Chapter 6

Tagged Without a Voice

There's something deeply unsettling about being spoken for.

Especially when what's said ~ or posted ~ doesn't match your experience. Children who are regularly featured in their parents' social media feeds are often painted in broad strokes. "My little champion." "Drama queen strikes again." "This one never listens." It might seem harmless. But it sets a tone. It tells a story.

And it's not always the child's story.

In my decades of teaching, I have seen this play out more times than I can count. Students come to school already burdened by the image others have of them. Not based on who they are in class, but on what has been seen online.

One girl confided in me that she stopped inviting friends over because her mum would take pictures of them and post about their "cute playdates" before the girls even finished playing. "I don't want to be a prop in her post," she told me, trying not to cry.

Another boy became the laughingstock of his year group when his dad posted a video of him practicing his dance moves in their lounge room. It was meant to be funny. But at school, it turned into mockery. Every hallway he walked through, someone was imitating the clip. He asked his dad to take it down. It stayed up for three more weeks.

Children are not just being seen. They are being assigned identities. "The sporty one." "The troublemaker." "The drama king." They are tagged in moments that feel like love but leave them feeling exposed. They are described in ways that box them in. And they are rarely given the chance to opt out.

Sharenting doesn't just record the moment. It interprets it. And once it's online, that interpretation becomes searchable. Permanent. Public.

As they grow, children begin to internalize these roles. Some become obsessed with living up to the version of themselves that gets the most likes. Others retreat into themselves, feeling unseen in the ways that really matter. And many ~ perhaps most ~ are simply confused. Why was this part of me shared? Why didn't anyone ask?

Many students, especially in their early teens, struggle to explain what this does to their sense of self. They carry the discomfort quietly. They scroll through their parents' feeds and feel disoriented. Whose life is this? Who gave it away?

They don't hate their parents. They don't always even bring it up. But inside, they are learning a quiet lesson about trust.

And trust, once fractured, is hard to piece back together.

Chapter 7

When Trust Starts to Fracture

There is a moment in many children's lives when the feeling of being loved begins to blur with the feeling of being used.

It's subtle. A child sees a post about themselves ~ maybe a story that paints them in a bad light or a silly photo they hoped had been forgotten. The caption is cheerful, playful even. But inside, the child feels reduced. Their vulnerability has been turned into a punchline. Their mistake into entertainment.

And somewhere deep inside, something begins to pull away.

Trust fractures in small, almost imperceptible ways. A child hesitates to speak up about something embarrassing, afraid it will end up online. A teenager starts keeping more of their thoughts private, protecting themselves not just from peers, but from the people who love them most. A relationship built on openness begins to close.

I've watched this erosion unfold over time. A parent proudly posts about their child's challenges, perhaps to raise awareness or build connection with others. But to the child, it feels like a betrayal. "Why would you share that?" they ask. The parent, often shocked, replies, "I just wanted people to know how strong you are."

But strength is not something you define for someone else. Especially not online. Especially not without permission.

In classrooms, I've seen the fallout. Students who once lit up now shrink when attention comes their way. Others overperform, trying to maintain the curated version of themselves their parents have shared. Some disengage altogether, feeling that nothing they do is truly theirs anymore.

These are not dramatic reactions. They are human ones.

When trust begins to fracture, what's lost isn't just a sense of safety. It's a child's confidence in their own agency. Their right to choose how their story is told. Their voice, their identity, their sense of control.

And those things ~ once lost ~ take years to rebuild.

Chapter 8

The Hidden Scars of Sharenting

Some impacts of sharenting are obvious. Embarrassment. Teasing. A moment of tension at home.

But others run deeper. Quieter. More permanent.

The hidden scars of sharenting are found in places most parents never see: the therapist's office. The school counselor's notes. The tear-streaked diary entry of a thirteen-year-old who feels like their life belongs to the internet.

I've read the journal entries. I've seen the emotional withdrawals. I've heard the quiet dread in a student's voice when they say, "I never know what she'll post next."

Some children begin to associate social media with anxiety long before they even have an account. They grow up in the spotlight of someone else's lens. Their baby photos, tantrums, bedtime routines ~ all shared. What they wear, what they eat, how they struggle ~ all catalogued. And when they begin to assert boundaries, they are often met with defensiveness. "But I'm your parent." "But it's my account."

But it's not just about ownership. It's about dignity.

41

Sharenting leaves scars in the form of shame. A child who sees themselves crying in a video captioned with laughing emojis does not feel seen. They feel mocked. A teenager who discovers an old post about their struggles with learning or behavior does not feel supported. They feel exposed.

Over time, these moments compound. They shape self-esteem. They influence how a child feels about being known.

Some hide. Some lash out. Some start to share excessively themselves, mimicking what they've seen and hoping to reclaim some form of control.

And in the most heartbreaking cases, they break. Social media becomes a trigger for isolation, identity confusion, and even self-harm.

These are not outliers. These are patterns. The emotional scars may not be visible, but they are deeply real. And they call us to pay attention.

Because every post about a child is more than a moment. It's a message. And that message, repeated enough times, becomes a belief.

Children deserve better. They deserve consent. They deserve care. And they deserve the chance to be the authors of their own story.

PART III: Public by Default ~ Privacy, Consent, & Digital Boundaries

#Don'tTagMe

Chapter 9

When Consent Isn't a Click

Consent is not a checkbox. It is not implied by a smile or the absence of protest. And in the digital lives of children, it cannot be assumed simply because they are too young to object.

In the world of sharenting, consent is often bypassed. Photos are taken. Stories are told. Videos are uploaded. All with the quiet presumption that because the parent has access, they also have the authority. But that assumption ignores a deeper truth ~ children are people, not content.

In many households, the conversation never happens. A child wakes up to find themselves featured in a new post ~ funny, vulnerable, perhaps even humiliating ~ with no warning, no invitation, and no way to remove it. When asked how they feel, some say nothing. Some say "I don't care." But that doesn't mean they weren't affected. It means they've learned not to speak.

As one study points out, "Parents rarely ask for their children's permission before sharing content, especially when children are very young" . The assumption of consent is deeply embedded in parental behavior online ~ even as children develop their own awareness of privacy, identity, and self-representation.

45

The gap between parent and child is not just technological ~ it is psychological. Parents often view their online posts as harmless, celebratory, or humorous. Yet children report feeling embarrassed, betrayed, or exposed . The intention may be love. The impact is something else.

In my experience as a teacher, I have seen firsthand how this disconnect plays out. A Year 6 student once confided in me, "My mum posted my report card before I even saw it." He wasn't angry. He was hurt. "I wanted to open it myself," he said, "not see it with a hundred comments already on it."

Another student, aged 14, burst into tears during a group assignment. When asked what was wrong, she said a boy in another class had shared an old TikTok her parents posted years ago ~ one that showed her crying during a tantrum. It had resurfaced as a joke, but it was never funny to her. She hadn't even remembered the clip until someone used it as a meme in their group chat.

This is the trauma of unspoken consent. It doesn't just erode trust. It fractures identity.

Children are learning that their story is being told for them. They are developing a sense of self through the lens of curated images and captions ~ none of which they approved. And increasingly, they are asking for a say. Research shows that by the time children reach adolescence, many express discomfort with how much of their lives have been shared without their knowledge .

Informed digital consent ~ the ability to say yes or no to what is shared ~ should be treated with the same seriousness as any other personal boundary. But for that to happen, we need to shift our lens as adults. We need to stop seeing our children as extensions of our online identity and start seeing them as the narrators of their own.

What if, before every post, we asked ~ "Do you want this shared?" What if we paused long enough to hear their answer ~ even if it's uncomfortable? What if their right to privacy outweighed our need for likes?

The legal systems are still catching up. But the ethical obligation is already here. And if we want to raise emotionally secure, self-aware children, we must start with a radical act of respect: asking first.

Because real consent ~ especially in the digital world ~ isn't about compliance. It's about dignity. It's about voice. It's about trust that isn't assumed but earned.

And once we begin to ask, we just might be surprised by what our children are ready to say.

Chapter 10

Digital Imprints and Future Identity

By the time a child turns five, they may already have hundreds of photos online ~ not uploaded by themselves, but by someone else.

The baby's first bath, the messy toddler tantrum, the first day at daycare, the cheeky quote during dinner ~ it's all there. Public, searchable, permanent. Long before they understand privacy, consent, or digital boundaries, their narrative is being formed for them.

In the past, children's identity development was a mostly private process. You tried on roles, experimented with preferences, failed in silence, and grew in the shelter of obscurity. Today's children grow up with an audience.

This audience ~ composed of family, friends, and strangers ~ doesn't just watch. It reacts. Likes, shares, comments. Feedback loops start early. A child learns what makes people laugh, what gets attention, and what kind of version of themselves is celebrated. That becomes a blueprint.

Psychologists have long understood that identity formation during childhood and adolescence is a delicate, complex process.

In the age of sharenting, this process can be compromised. Children may adopt personas that feel more performative than authentic ~ becoming the "funny one," the "naughty one," or the "inspirational overcomer" because that's what was reflected back to them again and again.

And when children eventually want to rewrite that story, they often can't. Their digital trail is already long. And they had no say in where it started or where it leads.

Research Evidence:

A 2024 systematic review of empirical literature on sharenting confirms the long-term identity risks for children exposed to high levels of online disclosure. The review concluded that children often experience "altered self-perceptions shaped by parental digital narratives," particularly when emotional content is shared without context or consent . Furthermore, Tosuntaş et al. emphasize that these early digital imprints may limit future identity exploration by locking children into predefined social roles .

Moreover, the paper *"Children's Privacy in the Age of Social Media"* highlights that digital identities are now often shaped externally rather than internally, leaving children vulnerable to "digital misrepresentation and psychological dissonance in later years" .

As teens, many struggle to separate who they truly are from how they were portrayed. A fourteen-year-old might find an old video of a meltdown posted when they were four and feel humiliated. A sixteen-year-old may discover a blog written by their parent detailing their behavioral challenges in early childhood. These moments do more than sting. They undermine autonomy. They shape reputation. And in some cases, they fracture trust.

Even efforts to reclaim the narrative are difficult. Platforms are not built for children to control their early digital footprints. Deleting old content is nearly impossible if you didn't post it yourself.

That means the first digital impression most people make ~ college admissions officers, employers, or new friends ~ may have come from their parent, not from them. A post intended to celebrate a milestone might one day become a barrier to opportunity.

This isn't about blame. Most parents don't foresee these outcomes. But that's precisely the point. The long-term impacts of sharenting aren't fully visible ~ yet they're increasingly unavoidable.

Research Evidence:

The 2023 UK-based study on Instagram-sharing behaviors of parents revealed that most parents underestimated the longevity and reach of their digital content. While 78% believed they were acting in their child's best interest, only 23% considered future identity implications. The gap between intention and consequence is clear, and it highlights the need for greater awareness and informed consent practices .

The question we must ask is simple but powerful: who owns a child's story?

Because if we keep writing it for them, we may be robbing them of the chance to become who they truly are.

Chapter 11

Platforms and Prompts

Social media was never neutral. It was never just a place to connect.

From the beginning, platforms like Facebook and Instagram were designed to prompt. To nudge. To suggest. They whisper in our digital ear with algorithmic precision: "Remember this moment from five years ago?" "Your memories are waiting." "Share what's happening now." A child's first steps, a sibling hug, a funny fall ~ it takes only seconds to capture, caption, and click "post."

But those prompts are not just reminders. They are engineered invitations. And they serve the interests of the platform, not the user.

What begins as a personal record quickly becomes public performance. The platform wants engagement. Parents want to share joy. The line blurs. We don't just remember the moment ~ we repost it. Again and again. We are cued to value our lives through a lens ~ and increasingly, through our children.

Most parents aren't trying to overshare. But they are being subtly guided to. Studies have shown that platform design, including automated memory prompts, photo resurfacing, and engagement rewards, play a significant role in habitual posting behaviors .

And once something is posted, it's no longer just yours. It lives on through shares, screenshots, reposts, and memories. Platforms capitalize on nostalgia, triggering emotional recall through algorithms that don't consider context or consent.

Research Evidence:

A 2023 study by El Asam and Caton explored how platform architecture influences sharenting behavior. It found that automated "memory prompts" (like Facebook's "On This Day" feature) increase the likelihood of re-sharing older content by 42%, even when the emotional relevance has diminished or when children have aged significantly since the original post . This reinforces a cycle of digital exposure, often without the child's knowledge or agreement.

In classrooms, we see the impact of these resurfaced memories. A Year 9 student once walked into class devastated because a baby photo had gone viral among classmates. It was resurfaced not because his parents reposted it intentionally, but because an algorithm prompted it ~ and they clicked.

These prompts create moments of emotional dissonance between generations. The parent feels nostalgia. The child feels exposure.

Even more concerning are the subtle shifts in behavior that platforms encourage over time. As engagement becomes a measure of validation, the pressure to share "engaging" content rises. Posts that include humor, embarrassment, or high emotion get more traction ~ and unfortunately, these often come at the child's expense.

Some parents begin posting updates not to connect with family, but to keep up with perceived social norms. Everyone else is sharing their child's dance recital. Everyone else is celebrating their teen's latest achievements. The platform amplifies this pressure. And children ~ often silently ~ carry the weight of that exposure.

Research Evidence:

According to a systematic review published in the *Journal of Family Theory & Review* (Tosuntaş, 2024), sharenting behaviors are "reinforced and amplified by platform-based nudges," creating a feedback loop that rewards emotionally vulnerable content and perpetuates parental oversharing habits . These patterns are not coincidental ~ they are embedded in the design.

If we are serious about protecting children's digital dignity, we need to begin by seeing these platforms for what they are: profit-driven ecosystems trained to harvest attention. They're not family photo albums. They're data engines.

That doesn't mean we can't use them. But it does mean we must resist their cues ~ and remember that not every memory needs to become media.

Because the real moment ~ the hug, the laugh, the story ~ already happened. And sometimes, the best way to honor it is to let it stay there.

Chapter 12

When the Digital Footprint Becomes a Shadow

Every person leaves a footprint online. But for today's children, many of those first footprints were left by someone else.

Photos taken at birth. Videos of tantrums. Medical updates. Funny stories. School wins. School losses. Year after year, a record builds. A footprint becomes a trail. And eventually, that trail becomes a shadow ~ one that stretches into places the child hasn't yet walked.

By the time some children create their first social media account, their digital identity is already deeply formed ~ not by them, but for them. And they begin to feel the weight of a version of themselves that was never theirs to author.

What happens when your online presence predates your memories?

Some try to reclaim the narrative. They ask their parents to take down old posts. Some parents do. Others refuse. They say things like, "It's my page," or "It's part of our family history." The child is left in a strange paradox: the subject of a public story they no longer own.

I've had students tell me they searched their own names and found dozens of images and quotes they didn't recognize. Some were mildly embarrassing. Others were deeply painful. And all of them were permanent.

Research Evidence:

In *Sharenting: Children's Privacy in the Age of Social Media*, Leaver, Highfield, and Abidin (2020) underscore this growing tension. They write, "Children are increasingly inheriting a digital identity not of their own making, often shaped by parental narratives that precede their capacity for consent or comprehension." These "legacy identities" can clash with a child's developing sense of self, leading to internal conflict and digital vulnerability as they enter adolescence .

The digital shadow doesn't stop at embarrassment. It influences how others see the child. Future peers, educators, employers, even strangers may encounter the curated history before they ever meet the person. And that curated history often lacks context, consent, or the opportunity for correction.

This is not a fear story. This is a cautionary one.

A child's online history may seem harmless in the moment. But as platforms evolve, as search tools improve, as digital archives deepen, what was once shared in innocence may one day be experienced as harm.

We do not yet know the long-term psychological impact of living with a digital past you did not create. But we do know this ~ every post we make about a child becomes part of that child's searchable memory.

Research Evidence:

The *Impact of Sharenting* report (2024) supports this concern, noting that "children often experience reputational consequences in adolescence based on parental posts made years prior, particularly when content was emotionally vulnerable, disciplinary, or body-related." These consequences manifest in reduced self-esteem, social anxiety, and identity confusion .

We must consider what we're handing over ~ not just to the internet, but to our children's future selves. Will they feel represented? Respected? Will they recognize themselves in the narrative we've left behind?

Because a shadow can offer comfort or it can obscure. And our task, as parents, teachers, and carers, is to ensure that whatever follows our children online ~ doesn't dim the light they are becoming.

PART IV: Behind the Screen ~ What & Why Parents Share

#Don'tTagMe

Chapter 13

Memory, Meaning, and the Modern Scrapbook

For centuries, families have passed down stories through photo albums, handwritten journals, and spoken word. Memory has always needed a container ~ a way to hold moments still before they vanish. In the digital age, that container became social media. For many parents, the impulse to share a moment online comes from a deeply human place: the need to document, to celebrate, to remember.

This chapter explores how the modern digital scrapbook ~ a parent's Instagram grid or Facebook timeline ~ often begins as a heartfelt expression of love and pride. A baby's first laugh. A messy first birthday cake. A proud photo in a school uniform. These posts are a way of freezing time, especially in the early chaos of parenting when days blur and milestones rush past.

But the line between memory-keeping and exposure is delicate. The emotional energy that fuels the post may be sacred ~ but the platform is not. Once shared, the image becomes part of a much wider ecosystem of clicks, likes, and algorithms. And with each upload, a parent creates a version of their child's identity that the child did not consent to ~ and may one day reject.

Memory is deeply emotional, and sharing can feel cathartic. It validates the hard work of parenting. It offers a sense of being seen in a role that is often invisible. And yet, the moment a memory is turned into content, its meaning subtly shifts. It becomes curated, shaped for an audience. Sometimes it's edited for humour or drama. Sometimes it's shared in the raw. But in either case, it now belongs to the public, not just the family.

Platforms encourage this. Facebook's memory feature, Instagram's story highlights, and even cloud storage reminders all invite us to relive and reshare. The digital scrapbook is no longer a private archive ~ it's a performance archive. And while it may begin with good intentions, it can slowly evolve into a narrative the child never asked for.

We ask an important question here: When does a digital scrapbook stop being a keepsake and start becoming a profile? Who benefits from the memory being public? And what role do social platforms play in turning moments of tenderness into marketable data?

As the child matures, these posts can influence self-perception. They may shape how a child is treated by peers, educators, or even by their own family members. A once-innocent anecdote or funny mishap, permanently accessible online, may become a source of embarrassment or even bullying. The permanence of the post gives it power that memory alone never held.

The answers aren't always clear. But the questions matter. Because the modern scrapbook isn't just a place to store memories ~ it's a place where children's lives are shaped, interpreted, and sometimes commodified, before they even understand what that means.

Chapter 14

Validation, Comparison, and the Performative Parent

Behind many sharenting posts is a story untold ~ a moment not of the child, but of the parent. In an age of curated lives, parents are not immune to the pull of validation. A sweet family moment that garners dozens of likes feels reassuring. A clever caption that sparks laughter in others feels connecting. Slowly, subtly, the act of sharing shifts from celebration to performance.

This chapter dives into the social psychology of parental sharing. We explore how digital platforms reward performative behaviors: the picturesque lunchbox, the immaculate family vacation, the bedtime selfie with a heartwarming quote. These posts do reflect real moments ~ but they also begin to shape what moments are chosen and how they're presented.

Validation is addictive. And in parenting, where affirmation is often rare, it can feel essential. A parent struggling with sleep deprivation or toddler tantrums may feel bolstered by a few supportive comments. But over time, the need for validation can lead to selective sharing ~ only the best, the funniest, the most moving. This turns the child into a kind of emotional currency.

Comparison creeps in. A mother who feels exhausted by tantrums might see another parent post a serene photo of a toddler meditating. A father might see photos of athletic trophies and wonder if his child is achieving enough. These silent comparisons ~ even when unconscious ~ can influence what is posted next. They may also contribute to parental anxiety, self-doubt, or a desire to overcompensate.

Children are perceptive. They notice what gets posted and what gets praised. They learn early which parts of themselves are "post-worthy." Some begin to perform for the camera, adjusting behavior for likes. Others withdraw, unsure if their natural selves are good enough.

Research confirms this pattern. A 2024 study published in *The Journal of Family Theory & Review* revealed that peer influence among parents plays a major role in posting decisions, a trend now known as "peer-induced sharenting" . The study also linked this behavior to increased feelings of pressure and competition, especially among mothers navigating early childhood parenting.

This chapter also considers the emotional impact on the parent. The pressure to keep up appearances online may add unnecessary strain to already challenging parenting seasons. What begins as an outlet for expression can spiral into a curated reality that feels difficult to sustain.

We are all vulnerable to needing connection. But when parenting becomes performative, the child's role changes too. They are no longer just the subject of a memory ~ they become part of the image-building process. And this, over time, can fracture trust. It can teach children that love must be photographed to be real, and that success must be public to be valid.

This chapter does not accuse. It reflects. It holds space for the uncomfortable truth that social media sometimes makes us say, show, and seek things we don't fully understand until years later.

Chapter 15

The Business of the Baby Photo

It is easy to forget that every post is a product.

Social media platforms do not just host your content. They monetize it. Every like, click, and share feeds into an algorithm designed to profile, target, and advertise. And when children are the content, the stakes are higher than most realize.

In this chapter, we confront the digital economy of sharenting. How baby photos become data points. How childhood milestones become content streams. And how parental influencers build entire brands around their children ~ often with no legal protection for the child's earnings or privacy.

One of the most striking realities uncovered in *Sharenting: A Systematic Review of the Empirical Literature* (Tosuntaş et al., 2024) is that children featured heavily in influencer culture have little to no control over their image rights, yet their likenesses are frequently commercialized without consent . These children often contribute significant income to family platforms without agency, protections, or even acknowledgment.

Even outside of influencer families, everyday parents contribute to this economy. Every tagged location, every hashtagged post, every story view provides data. That data is used to predict behavior, sell products, and feed a vast commercial infrastructure. We become not just users, but unpaid participants in a marketplace built around personal moments.

Further, research from the *UK-based study on sharenting and privacy (2022)* confirms that many parents remain unaware of how much metadata and visual content of their child is harvested and stored for commercial analysis . Despite privacy settings, content shared publicly or semi-publicly is often scraped and catalogued by third-party entities.

This commodification affects children in invisible ways. Their milestones ~ walking, talking, graduating ~ become content units. Their identities ~ sporty, silly, emotional, brave ~ become brandable traits. And their images, once shared, can circulate far beyond the family's control.

There are no clear guidelines, no safety rails. Laws regarding child influencers and digital labor are still evolving, and most countries lag behind the reality of how online platforms operate.

We ask in this chapter: What does it mean to commodify a child's life ~ even unintentionally? What rights do children have when their earliest digital footprints are owned not by them, but by tech companies and algorithms?

This chapter encourages a new lens: one that views each post not just as a memory, but as a potential transaction. And it asks us to pause before sharing, and to consider ~ not just what we're giving away, but who we're giving it to.

Chapter 16

The Platform's Pull ~ Designed to Keep You Sharing

Most parents do not begin their social media journey with the intent to exploit or expose their children. They begin with connection. With nostalgia. With joy. But the platforms on which we share are not neutral playgrounds. They are designed ecosystems ~ carefully crafted to guide behavior, extend engagement, and convert emotional expression into revenue.

In this chapter, we pull back the curtain on the subtle ways digital architecture encourages parents to keep sharing. The "On This Day" memory prompts, the quick emoji reactions, the view counters, the resharing nudges ~ these are not random. They are built to re-engage the user emotionally and behaviorally. For a parent feeling nostalgic, exhausted, or proud, the temptation to share "just one more" image is hard to resist.

Each time we post, we enter a feedback loop. Dopamine levels rise with likes, shares, and affirming comments. This neurological pattern ~ often associated with addiction ~ is well-documented in social media psychology. Platforms are designed to maximize this reward system, because the longer we stay, the more data they collect, and the more ads they can sell.

But when children are part of the shared content, this becomes more than a habit ~ it becomes a digital contract. The child's image, behavior, or story becomes part of the ongoing loop. Their identity is subtly shaped by algorithms that were never designed with their protection in mind.

Parents may not be aware of this manipulation. After all, the emotional logic of sharing is strong.

You feel proud, you post. You feel anxious, you post. You feel uncertain, you post. The platform rewards each of these moments with validation, gently reinforcing that sharing = connection.

Yet behind that emotional loop is a commercial one. What looks like a parenting tool is also a profit tool. What feels like memory-making is also data collection. And what we assume is a personal timeline is, in reality, a public-facing behavioral profile ~ one that includes our children.

This chapter does not seek to demonize platforms, but to illuminate design. It urges awareness. Because once we understand that the emotional pull of sharing is not purely organic, we regain power. And in doing so, we may choose differently. Pause more often. Share less impulsively. Or ask: "Is this memory mine to post, or theirs to keep?"

Chapter 17

When Sharing Heals and When It Harms

There are moments when sharing saves lives. When speaking the truth publicly dissolves shame, builds community, or opens space for collective healing. Parents facing grief, trauma, or chronic hardship often turn to social media for solidarity ~ and sometimes find it.

In this chapter, we explore the fine line between vulnerable expression and unintentional harm. The desire to be honest about postpartum depression, neurodivergent parenting, or childhood illness can be brave and connective. But when children are named, pictured, or tagged, their private lives become part of a narrative they did not shape.

The distinction lies in intention ~ and impact. Is the story shared to connect with others, or to draw validation? Is it anonymized and respectful, or raw and revealing? Does the child understand the context? Would they consent if they were older? These are not easy questions, but they are vital.

We also examine the phenomenon of trauma commodification: the rise of content that centers around pain and difficulty in order to gain visibility. While some parents share to process, others are unknowingly caught in algorithms that reward increasingly emotional or shocking content. This creates a dangerous dynamic: the more dramatic the post, the more engagement it receives.

Children are the unseen audience of this exchange. As they grow, they may encounter their own stories online ~ moments of illness, emotional breakdowns, or developmental diagnoses posted without context or consent. What feels brave to a parent may feel violating to a child. What seemed healing in the moment may echo as harm later.

There is also cultural nuance here. Some communities have long relied on shared storytelling for healing and connection. But even in those spaces, public storytelling must reckon with evolving definitions of privacy and autonomy.

This chapter offers a path forward. A framework for mindful sharing that honors both vulnerability and dignity. It encourages parents to check motivations, consider long-term impact, and invite consent whenever possible. It also celebrates the powerful act of private connection ~ the quiet message, the support group, the handwritten letter ~ as equally valid paths to healing.

Sometimes, the most respectful way to love a child is to protect their story ~ not because it's shameful, but because it's sacred.

#Don'tTagMe

Part V: The Why Behind the Post

#Don'tTagMe

Chapter 18

Memory, Meaning, and the Modern Scrapbook

For centuries, families passed down stories through photo albums, handwritten letters, baby books, and oral storytelling. Memory always needed a container ~ a vessel to preserve a moment before it slipped away. In the digital age, that container shifted dramatically. Today, it is most often a parent's Instagram grid, a Facebook timeline, a TikTok account, or a shared Google Photos archive.

The impulse to share a moment online often comes from a deeply human place: the need to document, to celebrate, to be witnessed in one's role as a parent. A baby's first giggle. A toddler's messy birthday cake. A proud school photo with a crooked tie. These are snapshots of love and belonging. They are also, increasingly, part of what researchers call "intimate surveillance" ~ a practice where digital sharing becomes a tool of memory, but also of identity shaping and emotional labor .

Memory, when shared, becomes collective. But it also becomes curated. The moment a photograph is posted publicly, it leaves the sacred space of family and enters an ecosystem governed by engagement, visibility, and algorithmic preference. A 2023 study on digital memory practices in the UK found that parents were often unaware of how platform design nudged them toward oversharing through reminders like "memories from this day," trending hashtags, or milestone prompt templates .

What begins as a digital scrapbook ~ a new version of the family photo album ~ can easily evolve into something more performative. Posts may be shaped to look spontaneous, but often they are carefully framed, filtered, and captioned for emotional resonance. Over time, the child becomes not just the subject of the memory, but a character in an unfolding narrative authored by someone else.

And children notice.

A growing body of research shows that many children begin to understand by early primary school that their image is being posted. Some begin to perform for the camera. Others pull away. A 2024 systematic review found that children's sense of autonomy is significantly impacted by repeated parental posting, especially when those posts are emotionally charged or meant to generate sympathy or praise .

There is no simple line between memory and exposure, between documentation and digital vulnerability. But the shift is worth pausing for. Because once a memory is posted, it is no longer just a memento ~ it is metadata. It is subject to data scraping, unauthorized circulation, and, perhaps most critically, a child's loss of narrative control.

Social platforms not only host memories ~ they prompt them, repackage them, and profit from them. Features like Facebook's "On This Day" or Instagram's "Story Highlights" encourage cyclical resurfacing of old posts, reinforcing what moments mattered ~ according to the platform. These are not neutral digital tools. They are commercial memory engines, and parents are both the authors and the unpaid content creators.

We ask, in this chapter, several questions worth sitting with:

~ When does a post shift from a keepsake to a claim?

~ When does a story told in love become a story imposed?

~ Who owns the memory once it's mediated by a platform?

The answers are not tidy. But they are essential.

Because the modern scrapbook is not kept in a drawer. It is public, searchable, and archived. And while the intention behind parental sharing may be rooted in connection, pride, or nostalgia, the outcome is increasingly complicated ~ especially for the children growing up inside that narrative.

As we move forward in this book, we invite readers to revisit their own digital scrapbooks with fresh eyes. Not with guilt or shame, but with awareness. Because memory is sacred ~ but visibility should be a choice.

Chapter 19

Validation, Comparison, and the Performative Parent

Why do we post? It's a question that echoes louder in parenting than almost anywhere else. In the early years of raising children ~ especially in the chaos of sleep-deprivation, routine change, and emotional overwhelm ~ connection matters. A like can feel like a lifeline. A comment can feel like a cheer. A post, carefully crafted or hastily shared, can feel like proof that we are not alone.

But underneath the sweetness of social approval lies a deeper reality: parenting has become performative. Not always intentionally ~ but steadily, inevitably, subtly.

This chapter explores the invisible ways social media reshapes the parenting experience. A baby's outfit photo isn't just a way to share joy. A caption about school drop-off chaos isn't just venting. Often, these are bids for validation, shaped by the logic of likes and the subtle pressure to appear engaged, happy, competent, or present.

Studies show that parents often begin sharing for memory-keeping or connection, but their behavior quickly shifts based on audience reaction. A 2021 qualitative study of British parents found that posts receiving more engagement influenced the kind of content parents continued to share, even if that content didn't fully reflect their real experiences . The curated version of family life slowly becomes the main version.

This is where performance begins.

A lunchbox photo garners admiration for creativity. A family holiday snapshot signals success. A funny toddler quote invites affirmation. Over time, these images aren't just shared for others ~ they begin to shape what parents capture, how they narrate their days, and which moments they elevate. It becomes a kind of social choreography. And the child, often unwittingly, becomes a co-star in that performance.

The emotional undercurrent here is powerful. Parenting is relentless. For many, it feels invisible. Social media offers a mirror. But it's a distorted one ~ angled to flatter, sharpen, and stylize.

This distortion matters. It teaches children that the parts of themselves most worthy of attention are the parts that perform well online. That authenticity may matter less than aesthetics. That silence means irrelevance.

Children observe. As educators have seen in classrooms across the world, many students now adjust their expressions, behavior, even their speech patterns when a phone is lifted. They know they're being watched ~ not by family, but by followers. In one study, researchers found that children as young as nine could articulate what types of posts about them felt acceptable versus invasive. Yet those preferences were rarely considered when content was shared .

Comparison exacerbates the issue. Peer-induced sharenting ~ the psychological phenomenon where parents post because others in their network are doing the same ~ creates a feedback loop of curated perfection. A parent sees a photo of a child winning a trophy and feels the sting of inadequacy. Another sees a serene family picnic and wonders why her family dinners end in tears. These comparisons are rarely spoken aloud. But they influence what we post next ~ and what we expect our children to deliver.

There's also a subtler risk. The line between our child's life and our own identity can blur. When a child's achievement becomes our validation, when their cuteness becomes our content, when their pain becomes our caption, we risk mining their life for emotional currency.

This doesn't mean parents are selfish. It means parents are human.

This chapter is not a critique. It is an invitation. To pause. To notice. To reflect.

What does our posting reveal about what we seek? Are we showing up as proud parents ~ or proving ourselves as competent ones? Are we sharing joy ~ or performing happiness?

In the end, the most meaningful parenting moments are often the ones no one else sees. The quiet reassurance. The messy triumph. The hard-fought repair after a hard day. These do not always translate to posts. But they build something deeper: trust.

And that, unlike a like, cannot be bought or broadcast. Only earned.

Chapter 20

When the Feed Becomes a File

We like to believe that social media is fleeting. Stories disappear in 24 hours. Posts get buried. Comments fade. But in truth, nothing online is ever truly gone. Every image, tag, and post contributes to something deeper ~ a data profile. What was once a simple photo shared between friends can quietly become a permanent part of a child's digital footprint.

This chapter explores how parental sharing contributes to long-term digital identity construction ~ and what that means for children growing into adults with no control over the narratives that shape them.

Most parents do not intend to create a file. They intend to share a moment. But with each click, tech companies harvest data: facial recognition markers, location tags, inferred interests, relationship patterns. In a 2020 report by the UK's Children's Commissioner, it was estimated that by the time a child turns 13, parents will have posted over 1,300 photos and videos of them online ~ often without their knowledge or consent. This unintentional archive forms what some researchers call a **digital dossier**, a permanent and expanding profile used by advertisers, data brokers, and sometimes future employers or institutions.

Even seemingly benign posts ~ a birthday photo, a family vacation, a school report ~ contain layered information. Geotags reveal home addresses. Background details show schools, routines, and even socioeconomic status. Algorithms, fueled by machine learning, can extract insights from this data at a level few parents understand. The feed, quite literally, becomes a file.

For children, this raises urgent concerns. Their digital identity is often established before they can walk. And as they age, they may struggle with a public version of themselves that doesn't reflect their private growth. A shy teenager may find a viral video from toddlerhood resurfaces, used by peers as a joke. A child questioning their identity may feel alienated by the curated images of their "younger self" that no longer feel authentic.

Research from Tosuntaş et al. (2024) in a systematic review on sharenting literature emphasizes this long-term impact. The review warns that sharenting not only affects current social dynamics but may also create emotional distress in adulthood when children attempt to assert boundaries that were never honored. The question becomes not just "Is this safe now?" but "What will this mean later?"

Some countries are starting to take notice. France, in 2023, proposed legislation that would require influencers to seek consent from children before monetizing content that features them ~ even suggesting that children could own image rights to their digital presence. But such protections are rare. Most legal frameworks treat children's online presence as an extension of parental freedom, not individual autonomy.

This chapter invites reflection. What happens when a parent's timeline becomes a permanent portfolio for their child? What are the emotional and ethical consequences of documenting a life before that life can speak for itself?

The answer is not to never share. It's to share with foresight. To understand that behind every upload is a digital echo. And that digital childhoods, like real ones, deserve protection, nuance, and privacy.

Because one day, that child will become an adult. And they may wish to rewrite their story. But the feed will already have told it.

Chapter 21

Consent in the Age of the Algorithm

Consent is a word that holds growing weight in our culture. We teach children to ask before touching someone's belongings, before entering personal space, before using someone's words or images. And yet, when it comes to posting about children online, that foundational respect for consent is often blurred or bypassed.

This chapter explores the evolving meaning of consent in a digital world ~ and how social media algorithms complicate what it means to say yes, or even to know what we're agreeing to.

Most parents do not consider themselves exploiters. When a photo is posted of a child dancing in the living room, the intent is usually joy, connection, or pride. But intent is only part of the story. The more complex question is: who gave permission? And can someone who doesn't yet understand the internet truly consent to being part of it?

A 2022 study published in *New Media & Society* found that many children between the ages of 10 and 13 were uncomfortable with photos shared about them online ~ yet most had never been asked. Even when children did voice discomfort, parents often dismissed it, citing parental authority or positive intentions. This mismatch reveals a troubling truth: digital consent is still framed through adult perception, not child autonomy.

In sharenting, the child is often invisible in the decision-making process. Their image is captured, edited, captioned, and uploaded without context. Their story is interpreted, often humorously or sentimentally, in ways they may not understand or agree with. While the child is legally a minor, emotionally and ethically, they are a subject ~ not just an object of parenting.

The algorithm adds another layer. Social media platforms thrive on content that performs well ~ especially content involving children. Posts featuring children often receive higher engagement, and platforms quietly prioritize them in feeds. This dynamic subtly encourages parents to post more, often without conscious awareness. The algorithm doesn't care about consent. It cares about reach, relevance, and revenue.

According to *Sharenting: Children's Privacy in the Age of Social Media* (Steinberg, 2017), the law has not kept pace with the emotional and ethical needs of children in digital spaces. While some countries enforce basic privacy protections, most still view children's online presence as an extension of their parents' rights, not as individuals with developing personhood.

And yet, child advocates are increasingly pushing back. In 2023, the United Nations Committee on the Rights of the Child issued a general comment affirming that children have a right to privacy in the digital environment. This includes the right to be consulted on how their data, image, and identity are used online. For many families, this will require a cultural shift: one in which children's voices are valued not only in person, but also in pixels.

This chapter asks us to reflect. Not just on what we post, but on how we model consent in a world where the line between personal and public is algorithmically blurred. How do we teach consent when we haven't practiced it ourselves? How do we invite children into conversations about privacy that we weren't taught to have?

Consent is not just a legal checkbox. It is a relational practice. And in the age of the algorithm, it is one of the most profound ways we can protect a child's dignity, voice, and evolving identity.

Chapter 22

The Hidden Curriculum of Exposure

Children do not just learn from the curriculum ~ they absorb the unspoken lessons embedded in everyday life. In education, we call this the *hidden curriculum* ~ the subtle messages students receive through school culture, expectations, interactions, and behaviors. But in today's world, a powerful part of that hidden curriculum lives outside the classroom ~ in the glow of a screen and the swipe of a feed.

Social media has become a parallel classroom. For many children, it is where values are formed, identity is shaped, and emotional norms are absorbed. And when parents share content about their children, knowingly or not, they are participating in a kind of informal curriculum of exposure.

What do children learn when their lives are constantly photographed and shared? What does it teach them when their emotional moments, private achievements, or personal struggles are turned into content?

Over 34 years of teaching, I've watched this silent curriculum unfold. I've seen students brush their hair, reapply lip gloss, and shift their body position just to catch the right angle before taking a photo in class. I've witnessed boys adjusting their clothing to make their bodies appear more dominant or visible for selfies. I've heard students talk in hushed tones about how their parents "posted again," often with visible embarrassment or frustration. These are not isolated moments. This is the landscape children are growing up in.

Students are internalizing that being seen matters more than being real. That a smiling photo means you're OK, even when you're not. That perfection wins attention. That exposure equals importance.

A 2023 study published in *Journal of Family Theory & Review* notes that children raised in high-exposure households often struggle to distinguish between public and private space. The boundary between "me" and "my image" becomes blurred. Some children begin to curate their lives for the camera ~ not just at home, but in school, friendships, and even play. Others retreat into silence, unsure of how to protect themselves from the constant lens.

This hidden curriculum teaches them to anticipate being watched, judged, or turned into a story. It disrupts authentic emotional development by introducing performance pressure where there should be trust and spontaneity.

And the implications are serious. Studies show that students who feel overexposed or surveilled are more likely to experience anxiety, social inhibition, and self-censorship in both academic and social settings (Tosuntaş, 2024). Their need for privacy becomes entangled with shame, and their right to control their own narrative is slowly eroded.

From my own experience, I remember one incident that changed the way I viewed exposure forever. As a volunteer photographer at a local community event, I took a group photo for the club's page ~ innocent, well-meaning, celebratory. Within 24 hours, a distressed parent contacted me. One of the children in the photo was involved in a custody battle and was meant to remain out of public view. The location, time, and appearance of that child were now visible online. I deleted the post immediately ~ but the digital footprint was already made.

That moment haunts me. It reminded me how quickly exposure can turn from joyful to dangerous. It reminded me that the camera doesn't just capture memories ~ it can create consequences.

This chapter invites us to reconsider what we're really teaching through our sharing. It challenges us to reflect on the silent messages encoded in every post: about identity, belonging, beauty, value, and safety. It urges us to teach children how to own their image, not perform for it ~ and to model that for them through our own restraint and respect.

The most powerful lessons are often unspoken. Let us ensure that the hidden curriculum of exposure is not one of overreach, but one of awareness.

Chapter 23

When the Law Lags Behind

The digital lives of children are unfolding faster than the laws meant to protect them. While institutions race to catch up with technological change, the lag between legal protections and real-world practices has left a gap ~ one where children's rights are quietly overlooked.

Parents are often unaware that once a child's image is uploaded to a platform, it becomes subject to that platform's terms of service, not just the family's wishes. In most jurisdictions, these images can be scraped, tracked, or reused without explicit permission, depending on platform policies. This makes the child's face ~ their identity ~ vulnerable to far more than their parents may have intended.

Legally, the child often has no say.

Globally, legislation surrounding children's digital rights is fragmented at best. In the United States, the Children's Online Privacy Protection Act (COPPA) was enacted in 1998, long before social media as we know it existed. It primarily focuses on businesses collecting data from children under 13, but does not address parental oversharing. Similarly, while the European

Union's GDPR includes protections for minors, enforcement remains inconsistent, and few parents understand how it applies to their own digital behavior.

A systematic review from Tosuntaş (2024) notes that "there is a significant legal vacuum regarding children's rights to control and delete digital traces left by their guardians" . The review highlights the lack of formal mechanisms for children to revoke consent for images posted during early childhood ~ a right increasingly argued for by digital rights activists.

As a teacher, I've witnessed this disconnect firsthand.

In one instance, a parent posted a photo of their child's award ceremony, tagging the location and including the full name of the school. What they didn't realize was that the child was currently part of a custody case, and their identity and whereabouts were legally supposed to remain protected. When another parent in the community recognized the child and notified authorities, the fallout was immediate. The image was removed, but not before it had been seen and potentially saved by dozens of others.

Another example involved a well-meaning parent who captured a group photo at a community soccer match. That photo included a student whose presence in the area was protected under a legal order. I myself had to delete a photo I'd uploaded to a club page for a similar reason ~ a simple post that almost compromised a child's safety. These mistakes are rarely intentional, but their consequences can be lasting.

The concern deepens with the rise of facial recognition technology. Even if a post is later removed, the metadata and facial features can remain indexed by third-party databases, invisible to the average user. A child's online presence becomes a permanent archive of data points that can be repurposed far into the future ~ for marketing, for tracking, or even for synthetic media without consent.

Current laws offer few remedies. In many countries, minors lack the legal agency to request deletion of content posted by their parents. There is also no formal accountability mechanism for parents who turn their children into digital brands, often generating significant income without compensation or consent.

As educators, we're expected to navigate this landscape delicately. But we receive little to no training on digital rights law, and policy directives often fall behind the rapid pace of tech innovation. The school system can implement opt-in forms and photography permissions, but what happens when a parent shares a picture from a school event that violates another child's privacy?

We're left to react, rather than prevent.

Chapter 23 calls for urgent legal reform. Sharenting is not simply a family matter. It is a civil rights issue. Children deserve the same protections online that they are afforded in the physical world. That means agency over their image, their data, and their digital footprint.

It also calls for education. Schools, parent groups, and policymakers must collaborate on clear, practical guidelines that uphold the child's right to consent, safety, and eventual control over their digital story. Because if the law continues to lag, the consequences will continue to fall ~ not on the platforms, but on the children caught in the crossfire.

Chapter 24

The Long Memory of the Internet

Children grow, change, and evolve ~ but the internet remembers them as they were.

This chapter addresses one of the most overlooked truths of our digital age: what we upload often stays, even when we believe it's gone. Unlike photo albums tucked away in drawers, a social media post has the potential to live forever ~ shared, saved, archived, scraped, re-uploaded, and embedded in places far beyond our original intentions.

For parents, this permanence is often misunderstood. A post made to mark a toddler's tantrum, a teenager's bad haircut, or a heartfelt family moment may seem harmless in the present. But that moment could be retrieved, reinterpreted, or resurfaced years later ~ during a college application process, a future job search, or even in the hands of someone with malicious intent.

A 2024 study published in the *Journal of Family Theory & Review* cautions that the digital trail left by parents through sharenting is "not only a present-day concern but an inheritance of digital identity" (Tosuntaş, 2024). Children inherit not only genetics and heirlooms ~ they inherit an online archive they did not curate.

As a teacher, I've had former students return as young adults only to tell me how their online pasts were raised during interviews or brought up by peers. One student, now in her early twenties, shared how a childhood photo posted by her parents ~ her face covered in chocolate and wearing only underwear ~ resurfaced on a meme page. She never gave permission. She never knew it had even been public. And she felt betrayed.

Another student, a quiet and academically gifted boy, once asked me if I could help him remove a video his parents had posted years earlier of him crying after losing a sports game. It had gone semi-viral in the local community and had become something people joked about. For him, it wasn't funny ~ it was humiliating. And yet, his digital presence had already outpaced his own ability to narrate his story.

The long memory of the internet teaches us that deletion is not always erasure. As noted in the article *Sharenting: Children's Privacy in the Age of Social Media* (Steinberg, 2017), digital footprints are often stored in cloud backups, browser caches, screenshot repositories, and third-party data collectors long after the original post is removed. Even platforms that promise "ephemeral content" may retain metadata or allow for undetected downloads.

What's more, the internet rarely forgets ~ but it often fragments. A child's digital identity can be scattered across platforms: photos on Facebook, videos on TikTok, mentions on school newsletters, and tagged images from friends and relatives. No single person, not even the parent, can fully track it.

This creates a fractured archive of the child's life ~ curated by others, searchable by strangers, and potentially accessible for decades.

This chapter challenges us to reframe the way we think about time online. Parenting is messy, emotional, and beautiful ~ but the digital documentation of that parenting must consider the child's future. Their privacy, their dignity, their ability to rewrite their own narrative depends on what we choose not to share as much as what we do.

Let us remember: the internet may offer quick validation, but it holds a long memory. The stories we post about our children may one day shape how the world sees them. More importantly, it may shape how they see themselves.

And when that day comes, will they say, "I'm glad you captured me"… or "I wish you had asked first"?

Chapter 25

Who Owns the Digital You?

In an era where personal moments are instantly shareable, the question of ownership has become both urgent and murky.

Who owns a child's digital identity when their image, story, and milestones are shared online without their consent?

➤ Is it the parent who clicked "upload"?
➤ The platform hosting the image?
➤ The advertiser targeting content to the viewer?
➤ Or the child, whose likeness and life are on display?

This chapter confronts a paradox of our age: while we champion children's rights in many areas, their digital identities often remain unprotected, owned more by platforms and parents than by the children themselves.

Social media terms of service reveal a hidden truth ~ when you upload an image to Instagram or Facebook, you grant the platform a broad license to use that content. While this doesn't mean outright ownership, it does mean the content can be stored, used, and analyzed long after you've deleted it. Algorithms don't forget. Data is archived, profiled, and commodified. In the case of sharented content, that data includes children's faces, interests, habits, and locations.

A 2024 review of empirical literature found that many parents were unaware of the extent to which platforms use this data. They saw posting as a personal action, not a commercial one . But platforms thrive on precisely this content ~ the informal, emotionally rich, real-life moments that increase user engagement and advertising value.

Legally, this space remains dangerously underregulated. In most jurisdictions, there are no specific laws granting children ownership over their digital footprints created by parents. While general data protection laws exist (like the GDPR in the EU), enforcement is inconsistent, and children's rights to erase or limit this content are difficult to exercise. Scholars have warned that this gap exposes children to long-term digital risks, including identity theft, psychological profiling, and exploitation .

There is also the issue of future consent. A child whose entire upbringing has been documented online may one day resent ~ or even be harmed by ~ content they had no role in approving. Their life has been interpreted and archived before they could speak for themselves. And while adults can curate their digital persona, many young people are forced to inherit one.

As a teacher, I have watched this unfold firsthand. I recall a high school student who, during a group assignment, asked why a photo of her in a tutu at age five still showed up whenever someone Googled her name. She was frustrated, not because the photo existed, but because it was posted by her mother with hashtags like #cutie and #dancerforlife. "That's not who I am," she said. "It never was." The photo had become a legacy ~ not of her talent or spirit, but of someone else's framing.

This isn't an isolated case. It's the consequence of a digital world where permanence is the default and consent is an afterthought.

We end this chapter with difficult but necessary questions:

➢ Should children have the right to request deletion of sharented content once they come of age?
➢ Should laws mandate financial and psychological protections for children featured prominently online?
➢ Should platforms be held accountable for content involving minors posted without explicit, evolving consent?

Until these questions are addressed at a legislative level, the responsibility falls on parents, educators, and digital citizens to ask ~ before we post: Who are we sharing this for? And who really owns what we've shared?

Chapter 26

The Algorithmic Parent

We like to believe that we are in control of what we post. That each caption, photo, and tag is a personal decision made with love, memory, or humor in mind. But beneath the surface of every social media post lies a network of subtle pressures ~ curated timelines, notification nudges, and emotional triggers designed not to serve our best interest, but to serve the platform's growth.

This chapter explores how parental posting is not just a personal act ~ it is a behavior shaped and reinforced by algorithms.

Social media platforms operate on engagement-based models. The more a user interacts, the more content is rewarded and seen. A simple birthday photo may receive hearts and comments. A vulnerable post about a parenting challenge might go viral. Over time, these feedback loops teach us which types of content 'work' ~ and many parents begin to subconsciously favor those types. This is not because they lack self-awareness or values ~ it's because they're being subtly trained by technology to optimize their own behavior.

This digital conditioning is especially potent in emotionally charged spaces like parenting. When your newborn's smile receives dozens of affirming reactions, it feels like community.

When your funny parenting anecdote gets reshared, it feels like validation. And when your child's award photo is applauded by others, it feels like a moment worth repeating.

But platforms don't just reward. They prompt.

"Memories from 10 years ago today…"

"Your post is getting more engagement than usual ~ boost it now?"

"Your friend just posted a photo ~ want to add yours?"

As you described from your own Facebook experience, these nudges often resurface old content unexpectedly, inviting you to update or repost. It's not malicious ~ it's part of a business model that thrives on re-engagement. But in the context of childhood photos, family updates, and identity evolution, these prompts can lead parents to repost content their children may no longer feel comfortable with.

Academic research supports this. A 2022 study by Kumar and Schoenebeck noted that platform design often drives "habitual oversharing," particularly among parents who initially used the platforms to connect with others during periods of social isolation or early parenthood. What begins as a lifeline can become a pattern, especially when combined with commercial incentives, such as brand recognition or affiliate links .

The result? The platform becomes a co-parent of sorts ~ not raising the child, but shaping how the child is represented to the world. And unlike a family member, the algorithm does not prioritize dignity, context, or long-term consequence. It prioritizes visibility.

As a teacher, I've seen this impact students directly. I recall one girl in Year 9 who refused to do a school project involving public speaking. When asked why, she finally admitted that a video of her reading aloud at age six had been shared to Facebook and mocked in the comments by distant relatives and strangers alike. Her mother thought it was adorable. For the daughter, it was humiliating. "Everyone saw it," she whispered. "Even people I'll never meet."

The algorithm had preserved a version of her that no longer matched who she was. But in the digital world, past and present are collapsed into a single timeline, with no expiration date unless someone actively removes it.

This chapter asks us to consider:

➢ What role do algorithms play in our parenting decisions?
➢ Are we curating our children's lives ~ or are we being curated by invisible code?
➢ Can we reclaim authorship over our own stories ~ and our children's ~ by resisting the prompts and pausing before we post?

The algorithmic parent is not a villain. It's all of us, shaped by systems we didn't design but now live within. Awareness is the first act of resistance.

Because before we hand over another photo, another moment, another milestone ~ we deserve to ask, "Who benefits from this ~ and who might it harm?"

#Don'tTagMe

Part VI: Reclaiming Boundaries ~ How to Move Forward

Chapter 27

Pause Before You Post

The simplest shift is often the hardest: taking a breath before sharing.

In the age of instant everything ~ instant news, instant photos, instant opinions ~ the act of pausing before posting may seem almost outdated. But for parents navigating the digital age, it's one of the most powerful tools we have. A pause creates space. Space to think. Space to reflect. Space to consider who we're really posting for ~ and who we might be posting *at the expense of.*

Most parents don't post with ill intent.

A cute video, a funny quote, a sports win ~ these are moments worth celebrating. And social media offers a convenient platform to do just that. But what happens when the moment shared is more about the adult's pride than the child's comfort? Or when it becomes content for public consumption rather than a keepsake for family connection?

This chapter invites a slow-down ~ a conscious moment between experience and exposure. That moment of pause is where digital parenting meets ethical responsibility.

Why Pause?

Because children grow. Because context changes. Because what feels harmless today might feel humiliating tomorrow. A post that once felt like a simple celebration might become a search result during a job interview, a source of shame during adolescence, or a remembered breach of trust between parent and child.

Psychologist Stacey Steinberg (2017) notes in her research on sharenting that "the more parents share, the less autonomy children have over their own digital identity." That pause ~ even if just five seconds long ~ is an invitation to protect your child's future self, not just document their present.

The Emotional Landscape of Posting

Often, the need to share is not just about the child, but about the parent. We post for validation, for connection, for a sense of being seen in the often invisible labor of parenting. These needs are real and understandable. But when they become habitual, when they eclipse our child's right to privacy, we risk reshaping our family stories around audience engagement rather than authentic experience.

Consider this: Are we posting because the moment is truly meaningful, or because we haven't been acknowledged in a while? Are we seeking likes, or are we longing for community? And can those needs be met in ways that don't involve our children's images or narratives?

A Mindful Framework: The Four-Part Pause

To support this shift, we offer a practical framework ~ four guiding questions that can help parents slow down and make more intentional choices online:

- ➢ **The Visibility Filter -** Who will see this, and how wide is that circle? Is the moment meant for close family, or is it being shared with acquaintances, strangers, or public platforms? Could this exposure affect my child socially, emotionally, or even legally down the line?
- ➢ **The Consent Check -** Would my child agree to this? If they're too young to understand, would their older self thank me for sharing it ~ or wish I hadn't? A hesitation is often a sign that more reflection is needed.
- ➢ **The Emotional Audit -** What am I feeling right now? Am I posting from joy, or from overwhelm, comparison, frustration, or the need to prove something? Digital emotion is fast ~ but parenting values are slow.
- ➢ **The Legacy Lens -** How might this post age? Will it feel protective and respectful years from now? Could it be misinterpreted, taken out of context, or weaponized? If my child found this post as a teenager, how would they feel?

Parent Voices: Learning to Pause

Many parents who've adopted a pause-first approach describe it not as restrictive, but freeing. One mother wrote: *"I used to post everything. Now I write a caption, sit with it for a day, and usually end up saving it to a private folder instead. It still counts as a memory. Just not one I owe the world."*

A father reflected: *"It's not about fear. It's about dignity. My daughter is hilarious, but some of her moments are just ours ~ not for the algorithm."*

Rebuilding Digital Trust

If your child is old enough, consider making the pause a shared process. Ask them how they feel about being included in a post. Let them choose the photo. Invite their voice into the caption. These small gestures build long-term trust. They teach children that their image belongs to them ~ not to an app.

And if your child is too young to give consent, let that be your cue to protect more, post less, and choose privacy as a form of love.

In Summary

The pause is not a rejection of memory-making. It is a return to intention. A parent who pauses is not less loving ~ they are more mindful. In a culture that encourages oversharing, the decision to stop and think is a radical act of respect.

It says: *I see you, and I will not let the world decide who you are before you get the chance to.*

Chapter 28

Consent Starts at Home

Consent is not just a legal checkbox ~ it's a relational practice. And in families, especially those raising digital natives, consent must begin earlier and run deeper than many of us were ever taught. This chapter is a call to embed the concept of consent into everyday life ~ not as a one-time "talk" but as an evolving conversation built on trust and mutual respect.

For too long, the assumption has been that parental consent is sufficient to post images or stories of children online. But this framework overlooks a critical truth: parents themselves are often the primary creators and curators of their child's digital footprint. And yet, the child ~ the person most affected ~ is rarely given a voice.

Children deserve a say in their digital lives. Even if they are too young to understand the consequences, they are still people in development ~ worthy of privacy, dignity, and boundaries. The earlier we practice asking, listening, and respecting their comfort, the more likely they are to carry those same values forward in their own lives.

The Roots of Digital Respect

The most powerful lessons in consent don't come from lectures ~ they come from how we live. When we pause before posting.

When we ask, "Would this embarrass you?" When we give children the choice to say no, even if we think the photo is adorable or funny or heartwarming. These moments build something deeper than compliance ~ they build self-respect and relational trust.

Children who grow up being asked for their input about what gets shared about them learn that their voice matters. They begin to internalize that their body, image, story, and boundaries belong to them.

A Family Practice: Creating a Digital Boundaries Agreement

One of the most helpful tools I've encountered is the idea of a family digital boundaries agreement. This isn't a rigid contract or punishment system ~ it's a shared understanding, co-created between parents and children to guide how we navigate our online lives together.

Such an agreement might include things like:

➢ "You'll ask me before posting photos that include me."
➢ "If I say I don't want something shared, you'll respect that."
➢ "We'll talk together about which kinds of posts are OK and which are private."
➢ "When emotions are high, we wait 24 hours before posting anything."

These agreements evolve with age. For toddlers, it's about me as a parent developing awareness. For school-aged kids, it's about starting the conversation. For teens, it's a mutual commitment to digital respect.

A 2024 study in the *Journal of Family Theory & Review* (Tosuntaş, 2024) supports this approach. It found that children who were involved in digital boundary conversations reported higher trust in their parents, increased digital literacy, and lower levels of resentment toward past sharenting. The act of co-creating boundaries, rather than imposing them, creates space for growth, not guilt.

My Personal Story: Leading by Imperfect Example

I've lived this journey from both sides. As a parent and a teacher of 34 years, I've witnessed the power ~ and the pitfalls ~ of sharing.

I started using Facebook back in 2008. My family was active, sporty, and we travelled a lot. I was like many other parents. I shared grand final wins, beautiful scenery from our overseas adventures, silly videos of our pets doing ridiculous things. It felt innocent ~ joyful, even. Social media was simply a digital scrapbook where I could celebrate my kids and our life together.

But over time, I noticed something shift. Platforms began prompting me to post. Facebook would send me a "memory" and say, *That was then. What about now?* One day, I followed the prompt and posted a "then and now" image of my children. It was a tender moment for me ~ a reflection of how fast they'd grown.

But when my child saw it, they said, *"Why the hell did you post that, Dad?"*

That moment stopped me. It didn't just sting ~ it woke me up. What I saw as nostalgia, they saw as overexposure. What I thought was a harmless post felt, to them, like a breach of privacy.

Since then, I've become far more cautious. I no longer post automatically. I delete more than I share. I think about the *why* before I post anything about my family. And more importantly ~ I ask.

From Ownership to Stewardship

The concept of digital consent forces us to rethink something fundamental: that our children's lives are not extensions of our own. We are not owners of their stories ~ we are stewards. Our job is not to control the narrative, but to protect the space until they are ready to write it themselves.

Social media makes it easy to forget this. But our children remember. They may not say anything now ~ or they may say it loudly. Either way, the trust we build or break today will echo for years.

In Summary

Consent starts at home. Not just because it's the right thing to do ~ but because it's a foundation for every future relationship our children will have: with themselves, their peers, their bodies, and their boundaries.

If we want our children to grow into adults who respect privacy, speak up for themselves, and ask before they act ~ we must start modeling those values now.

And it starts with a pause. A question. A conversation.

Chapter 29

The Moment They Say "Stop"

There's a moment in every parent's digital journey that can feel like a slap and a gift in the same breath.

It might come quietly ~ a muttered "Don't post that."
Or abruptly ~ "Take it down. Now."
Or even years later, through a pained expression, "I hate that you put that online."

This chapter is about what we do next.

For many parents, that first boundary set by a child is unexpected. It collides with years of intention: the joy of sharing milestones, the belief that you were documenting love, pride, and connection. When a child says "stop," it can feel like rejection. But beneath the sting is something precious ~ a moment of awakening, and a door to deeper respect.

Why It Feels So Personal

Children asking for digital boundaries can trigger a surge of emotions. Guilt. Embarrassment. Defensiveness. A quiet panic that says, "But I didn't mean to hurt you."

It helps to understand that these reactions aren't wrong ~ they're human. According to research in parent-child digital dynamics (Tosuntaş, 2024), most parents believe they are acting out of love when they post. But love doesn't always translate to comfort for the child. The disconnect is not in affection, but in agency.

The shift required in this moment is from intention to impact.

Learning to Hear What They're Really Saying

When a child says "I don't want you to post that," they're not just making a digital request. They're expressing a need for ownership over their body, their image, their story. They're testing whether their voice matters.

Responding with "But I already posted it," or "Everyone does it," may unintentionally invalidate their need for control. Instead, we can slow down and ask ourselves:

➢ Am I hearing their discomfort, or just my own surprise?
➢ Can I pause my defense long enough to hear their boundary?
➢ What would it mean to value their no?

What Listening Looks Like

Research shows that children who feel heard in moments of digital conflict are significantly more likely to engage in healthy boundary-setting later in adolescence (Brosch & Glowacz, 2021). Listening might mean:

> ➢ Taking the post down without resistance.
> ➢ Letting them explain why it made them uncomfortable.
> ➢ Acknowledging that you didn't realize it was hurtful.
> ➢ Asking how they'd like to handle future posts.

These moments rebuild trust. They tell the child: "You matter more than the post."

My Turning Point

I remember the first time one of my children directly challenged me on a post. Facebook had prompted me with a "memory" and I'd shared a throwback without hesitation. It was a photo of a younger version of them ~ funny, sweet, unfiltered. I saw nostalgia. They saw exposure. Their reaction was blunt: "Why the hell did you post that, Dad?"

It was a jarring moment. Not because they were rude ~ but because I had genuinely thought the image was harmless. That moment became a marker in my parenting timeline. It forced me to consider that my love for the memory didn't give me permission to make it public.

Since then, I've taken more time to reflect. I ask before I post. I don't assume a funny face or childhood blooper is fair game. The boundary, once drawn, became a guidepost for something greater: mutual respect.

The Gift in the Discomfort

When a child says "stop," they are not shutting us out. They're inviting us in ~ to a deeper kind of relationship, one built not on ownership but on partnership. They are learning to say no, and in doing so, learning how to protect themselves.

And we, in turn, get to learn what it means to parent in a world where visibility is no longer a gift ~ but a choice.

In Summary

These moments are tender. They're charged. And they matter more than we often realize at the time.

To hear your child say "stop" and to honor it ~ even when it's hard ~ is to show them that they are more than a photo, more than a story, more than your memory of them.

They are a person. Becoming.
And your job is not to post their story, but to protect their right to tell it.

Chapter 30

From Performative to Protective

It starts with a click. A smile. A beautiful moment between you and your child, caught in perfect light.

The instinct to share is immediate. But so too is the opportunity to pause.

This chapter invites that pause.

Not as a reprimand ~ but as a return to purpose.
From performative to protective. From showcasing your child to safeguarding their story.

How Sharing Becomes Performing

In today's culture of oversharing, the line between celebration and performance is often blurred. Platforms are built to reward engagement ~ the likes, the shares, the quick dopamine hits that come with digital approval. It's easy to forget that your child's image isn't just capturing a moment ~ it's entering a marketplace.

Studies confirm this shift. In *The Impact of Sharenting* (Donovan, 2023), researchers found that parents often began sharing as a way to document, but slowly felt drawn into cycles of curated storytelling. The more engagement posts received, the more pressure was felt to maintain that narrative.

Even outside of influencer culture, everyday parents begin crafting a family brand ~ happy, successful, connected. The images are real, but the selection is intentional. The gaps, the messiness, the moments when children say no or cry or resist ~ they stay offline. This imbalance subtly teaches children that only their polished selves are share-worthy.

The Shift Toward Protection

Becoming protective doesn't mean disappearing. It means realigning your role.

Where once we asked:
"How will this post be received?"
We now ask: "Does this honor my child's privacy and dignity?"

A protective posture invites a different set of questions:

> ➤ Have I asked my child's permission?
> ➤ Am I sharing this for connection, or for approval?
> ➤ Could this content embarrass them in five years?
> ➤ Would I be okay with this being shown in their classroom? Or job interview?

Creating a Pause Practice

Protection is not about silence. It's about discernment. You can still celebrate, document, connect ~ but with filters rooted in consent and respect.

A simple pause practice might look like this:

> ➢ **Reflect**: Who benefits from this post?
> ➢ **Assess**: Is this moment sacred or sharable?
> ➢ **Ask**: Have I checked in with my child, if they're old enough?
> ➢ **Consider**: Does this image feed connection ~ or performance?
> ➢ **Decide**: Is there another way to document this memory ~ privately?

What Protection Looks Like in Action

It looks like parents disabling tags on their child's photos.

It looks like switching profiles to private, or better yet, archiving past content.

It looks like conversations with grandparents and friends about what can and cannot be shared.

It looks like saying "no" to a photo, even if it's beautiful, because your child isn't comfortable.

And it looks like children growing up knowing that their parents would rather protect them than promote them.

The Long Game: Trust

Performative parenting gives us moments. Protective parenting builds a foundation.

When children know their voices are heard, their images are guarded, and their stories are treated with care, they grow up trusting that their personhood is valued. Not for how cute they looked online. Not for how funny their meltdown was on video. But for who they are, quietly, day to day.

This trust is not built through one perfect decision. It's built over time ~ through a thousand quiet choices to pause, to ask, and to protect.

In Summary

To move from performative to protective is to reframe your role in your child's digital world. You are not their publicist. You are their guardian.

Not just of their physical safety, but of their dignity, their consent, and their unfolding identity.

Chapter 31

Through Their Eyes ~ What Kids Wish We Knew

For all the talk about parental rights, digital legacy, and safety, there's a voice we too often overlook: the child's.

This chapter steps inside the mind of the young person ~ the child who becomes the content. The teenager who has lived their whole life online before they could spell "privacy." The student who learns more about themselves from their mother's blog posts than from self-reflection. These are not abstract ideas. They are lived experiences.

Young people are not just digital natives ~ they are digital survivors.

As adults, we may share out of pride, joy, or even concern. But what does the child feel? What do they *wish* they could say about their lives being posted, filtered, tagged, and liked?

Many young people say nothing. Not because they don't feel it, but because they know they can't compete with a parent's authority or social visibility. Others whisper to friends, laugh it off, or quietly delete tags and unarchive images. Some ask for photos not to be shared ~ only to see them posted anyway.

A 2022 UK-based study interviewed children aged 10 to 17 and found that many were deeply uncomfortable with how their parents shared images of them online. Their discomfort ranged from embarrassment about awkward or vulnerable photos, to fears about future consequences like college admissions or job prospects. Some simply didn't feel like their image belonged to them anymore.

Other research highlights how young people see their online identities as extensions of self. When a parent posts without asking, it can feel like a personal violation. This is especially true during adolescence ~ a time when identity formation is both sacred and fragile. Digital overexposure can lead to increased anxiety, identity confusion, and loss of agency.

And yet, children rarely feel empowered to say no.

In one study, participants said they wished parents would "ask first," "respect a no," and "understand that some moments are just for family, not followers." One teenager, age 15, said: "I'm not a character in your story. I'm trying to figure out mine."

That quote captures the essence of this chapter. Children are not props. They are people.

We must ask: Are we listening?

Because when we do, the message is clear: They want boundaries. They want agency. They want their childhoods back.

Student Story
"I Found Out Who I Was on Mum's Blog"

A Year 10 student once came to me after a lesson on digital identity and privacy. She asked if she could stay behind for a chat. Her voice was calm but held back something deeper.

"I Googled my name last night," she said. "My mum has a parenting blog. I found a post about when I used to self-harm. I didn't even know she told anyone. She never asked."

She wasn't angry in that moment ~ just quiet. Flat. Not surprised.

She told me she had been in Year 7 when the post was written. "She meant well," she said, "but now it's there. Forever. That's not how I want people to know me."

She hadn't told her mum that she found it. She didn't feel she could. Instead, she avoided family events where photos might be taken. She turned her Instagram to private and blocked several extended family members. She began speaking in class less. Watching more. Shrinking a little each term.

I saw firsthand how digital exposure, even when well-intentioned, had reshaped her trust in adults.

She wasn't looking for punishment. She was longing for protection.

Her story is not an outlier.

Many students, especially those in upper primary and high school, begin to question why their images are online. Some even discover that their baby photos are more searchable than their resumes. Others learn about their mental health history or childhood struggles not from a private conversation, but from a blog post their parent shared years ago.

That story was never hers to tell ~ but it was told.

When children say "Don't post that," it's not rebellion. It's self-protection. It's an invitation to be seen as someone with the right to their own narrative.

And when we as parents, educators, or carers respect that, something powerful happens. Trust is rebuilt. Autonomy is restored. Identity becomes something children create for themselves, not something assigned by algorithms or parental nostalgia.

Let this chapter be a listening room. Not a lecture.

What kids want us to know is simple:

➢ Just ask first.
➢ Don't post when emotions are high.
➢ Let them say no.
➢ Be open to being wrong.
➢ Understand that privacy is love.

If we want to raise confident, self-aware young people, we must first learn what it feels like to hand them back their voice.

They've seen enough. Now let them speak.

Chapter 32

The Parent-Child Digital Agreement

In every relationship, boundaries create safety. In parenting, boundaries can feel blurry ~ especially in the digital age where love, pride, and protection sometimes get tangled in the act of sharing. That's why this chapter offers a practical step forward: a Parent-Child Digital Agreement.

This is not a contract for punishment. It's a framework for conversation.

The idea is simple but powerful: What if, before posting, parents and children talked about what mattered to both of them online? What if families made decisions together about how, when, and whether to share personal moments? What if digital dignity became a shared value?

Agreements like these are already used in homes across the world to address things like screen time, gaming limits, and phone usage. But rarely do we see one focused on the *act of posting* ~ and the emotional, social, and legal consequences that come with it.

We believe this kind of agreement is the next evolution of digital parenting.

Drawing from family systems psychology, social-emotional learning, and child privacy law, the Parent-Child Digital Agreement is built on five foundational pillars:

> ➢ **Consent**: No post or photo is shared without the child's permission, regardless of age.
> ➢ **Context**: What's okay to share publicly? What's just for family? What's off-limits entirely?
> ➢ **Control**: The child can ask for a post to be removed ~ and it will be.
> ➢ **Check-ins**: Regular, scheduled conversations to revisit the agreement as the child grows.
> ➢ **Compassion**: An understanding that mistakes will happen ~ and repair is always part of the process.

These aren't just guidelines. They're relational commitments.

Creating this kind of agreement together sends a powerful message to your child: *I trust you to have a voice. I respect your boundaries. I am still learning, too.*

And the process of making the agreement matters just as much as the outcome. Some families do this around the dinner table. Others create a digital document or journal it out. However it's done, it becomes more than just rules ~ it becomes a living conversation about identity, trust, and emotional safety.

Here's what one version might look like:

Sample Parent-Child Digital Agreement

We agree that:

➢ I will always ask before sharing your photo or story online.
➢ You have the right to say no, and I will respect that.
➢ We will decide together what types of moments are okay to share and which are private.
➢ You can always ask me to delete something, and I will. No questions, no guilt.
➢ We will have regular check-ins to update this agreement as you grow.
➢ This is a space for honesty, not blame. We are both learning.

Signed:
Parent(s) Name: _____
Child's Name: _____
Date: _____

This kind of agreement can evolve as children mature. A six-year-old might simply say "no bath photos." A fifteen-year-old might request that you don't tag them without asking. The goal is not perfection ~ it's partnership.

Research Connection: A 2023 study published in the *Journal of Child and Family Studies* noted that children who participated in family agreements around digital technology reported higher levels of trust, lower stress, and stronger communication within the home. The same study found that when children's preferences about sharing were honored, their self-esteem and sense of agency improved measurably.

From Personal Experience: I've witnessed how easily trust can be fractured in digital spaces ~ and how powerful it is when children feel like collaborators instead of content. I've seen the emotional relief when a child realizes they *can* say no to a post ~ and be heard.

➤ This agreement isn't a fix-all. But it is a beginning.
➤ It's a pause button in a world that's always rushing to upload.
➤ It's a mirror held up to our intentions.
➤ It's a tool that says: *Your story is yours, and I want to honor that.*

Chapter 33

What If We Get It Right?

We've spent this book shining a light into the hidden corners of sharenting ~ the unintended harm, the digital risks, the emotional toll. But we close now with possibility.

What if we get it right?

What if the next generation of parents raises children who are digitally seen only with permission ~ not performance? What if families become known not for how much they share, but for how deeply they listen? What if dignity becomes more important than documentation?

This chapter imagines that future.

It's a world where photo albums return to private shelves, or locked cloud drives. Where the beauty of childhood lives in memory, not in metrics. Where teenagers feel trusted to tell their own stories, and not pressured to live out the ones we published for them before they could even speak.

It's also a world where schools teach digital empathy as rigorously as they teach literacy. Where child protection laws

include clauses for consent and image rights. Where algorithms are redesigned not just to engage, but to protect.

We envision parents who pause before posting, who ask before tagging, who honour their child's unfolding identity as sacred ~ not social content. And we imagine children growing up with fewer shadows to outgrow, and more agency to build their online legacy in their own time.

This isn't naïve hope. It's a reachable future.

The technology is already here. The research is growing. The awareness is rising. What's needed next is courage. The courage to resist the cultural tide of oversharing. The courage to let our kids grow up without the camera always rolling. The courage to apologise when we've gone too far, and to do better tomorrow.

We will make mistakes. We already have. But we can change course. The digital world is editable ~ and so is our parenting in it.

This chapter invites you not to retreat from digital life ~ but to move through it with reverence. With curiosity. With boundaries. With the fierce and tender love of someone who knows their child's story is not theirs to tell ~ but theirs to protect.

PART VII: Legacy & Leadership

#Don'tTagMe

Chapter 34

What Will They Remember?

My Reflection as a Teacher and Parent

My teaching, and a lifetime of parenting, have taught me more than any research paper ever could. But when experience meets evidence, something powerful happens ~ perspective deepens, and patterns become impossible to ignore.

In the early 2000s, I celebrated like many others did. My children were winning grand finals, we were off on adventures, and I loved posting silly videos of our pets and beautiful travel photos on Facebook. It felt harmless, joyful, even connective. But somewhere along the way, I started to see things differently.

One moment stands out clearly. Facebook prompted me to post a "then and now" photo of my children. It offered up an image, full of nostalgia for me, and I clicked 'share' without much thought. The response from my child was swift: *"Why the hell did you post that, Dad?"*

That reaction was more than discomfort ~ it was a boundary. I had crossed a line I didn't even know existed.

Teaching, I've seen this boundary crossed too many times.

I've watched children shrink in the classroom after classmates passed around embarrassing posts their parents had shared. I've sat with students in tears after a well-meaning parent uploaded a meltdown video, captioned with a joke, and it went viral in their school circle. One child, whose face appeared in a community club post I had shared (without realizing they were under protective custody), triggered a legal emergency. That single post made me re-evaluate every digital habit I had.

What do they remember? Not just what we post, but how we respond when they ask us not to.

According to a 2024 systematic review, children of highly active sharenting parents reported increased anxiety about peer perception, reduced feelings of safety, and concerns about not being in control of their public identity . Another study of UK parents found that the vast majority had never asked their child's permission to post, even though 42% of the children expressed discomfort with what had been shared .

The long-term social-emotional impacts aren't abstract anymore. They're evident in withdrawn behavior, in mistrust between parent and child, and in subtle identity confusion ~ "Am I the person I really feel like, or am I just the version they share online?"

But I've also seen healing.

I've seen students open up when their parents began asking for consent. I've seen trust restored when old posts were taken down. I've seen kids glow when they were allowed to tell their own stories in their own time.

Presence is the answer. Not performative presence for the platform, but embodied presence ~ the kind that looks your child in the eyes and listens. The kind that protects their becoming rather than narrating it online. The kind that resists the urge to share, even when the photo is perfect.

They'll remember that. They'll remember that you saw them, not just posted them.

Chapter 35

The "Don't Tag Me" Manifesto

A Cultural Pledge of Digital Dignity

This chapter is not a conclusion. It's a beginning.

The *"Don't Tag Me" Manifesto* is our collective promise to move differently. To resist the automatic upload. To remember that our children's stories are theirs ~ not ours to edit, brand, or broadcast.

The Core Pledge:

- ➤ My child is not my content.
- ➤ I will ask before I post.
- ➤ I will honour their no without guilt.
- ➤ I will remove digital media when asked.
- ➤ I will reflect before I share.
- ➤ I will lead by example.

This is not about shame. It's about sovereignty. About reclaiming boundaries that have been quietly eroded by likes, algorithms, and culture.

Children raised under constant digital surveillance are more likely to experience privacy confusion, a diminished sense of ownership over their image, and blurred personal boundaries. Research from *The Journal of Family Theory & Review* warns that the child's "emerging self-concept may be shaped more by online narrative than by internal experience" .

We cannot wait for governments to legislate morality. We must lead now.

Let this manifesto be read aloud in homes. Let it be printed on the fridge, agreed to as a family, and shared not as content ~ but as commitment.

The Vision Forward:
- A world where parents seek permission as often as they seek praise.
- A world where digital empathy is as important as digital access.
- A world where children's stories remain sacred until they are ready to be told.

When we shift from "Look at my child" to "I see you, child," we change everything.

Let this be the moment we begin again ~ not more silent, but more sovereign. Not less connected, but more conscious.

Because parenting is leadership. And leadership means knowing when not to post.

Endnotes

➤ Blum-Ross, A., & Livingstone, S. (2017). Sharenting, Peer Influence, and Privacy Concerns: A Study on the Instagram-Sharing Behaviors of Parents in the United Kingdom. London School of Economics and Political Science.

➤ Blum-Ross, A., & Livingstone, S. (2017). The Trouble with "Sharenting". The Atlantic.

➤ Leaver, T. (2020). The Impact of Sharenting: Children's Rights, Digital Media, and the Public/Private Boundary. Media International Australia.

➤ Tosuntaş, Ş.B. et al. (2024). Sharenting: A Systematic Review of the Empirical Literature. Journal of Family Theory & Review.

➤ Kumar, P., & Schoenebeck, S. (2015). The Modern Digital Scrapbook: How Parents Use Facebook and Instagram for Memory Keeping. Proceedings of CHI.

➤ Choi, G.Y., & Lewallen, J. (2021). Social Media and Adolescent Development: Risks, Opportunities, and Guidance for Families. Journal of Adolescent Health.

➤ Steinberg, L. (2014). Age of Opportunity: Lessons from the New Science of Adolescence. Houghton Mifflin Harcourt.

➤ Amanda Todd (2012). My Story: Struggling, Bullying, Suicide, Self Harm and the final outcry of help https://www.youtube.com/watch?v=vOHXGNx-E7E

139

➢ Amanda Todd's Video Description (2012). "I'm struggling to stay in this world, because everything just touches me so deeply..."

➢ Marwick, A., & boyd, d. (2014). It's Complicated: The Social Lives of Networked Teens. Yale University Press.

➢ Hiniker, A., & Schoenebeck, S. (2020). Not My Kids: Parents' Perceptions of Children's Online Privacy Risks. Proceedings of ACM CHI Conference.

➢ Office of the eSafety Commissioner (Australia). Children's exposure to sharenting and image-based abuse. www.esafety.gov.au

➢ Office of the Australian Information Commissioner (OAIC). Privacy and Your Rights: A Guide for Parents and Carers.

➢ Australian Government. (2024). Online Safety Amendment (Protecting Children) Bill.

➢ Livingstone, S., Mascheroni, G., & Staksrud, E. (2018). European research on children's internet use: Assessing the past and anticipating the future. New Media & Society.

➢ Ghosh, S., & Banerjee, R. (2022). Digital Footprints of the Innocent: Long-Term Effects of Online Childhood Exposure. International Journal of Child Rights & Technology.

Academic Resource Summaries

1. Title: Sharenting, Peer Influence, and Privacy Concerns: A Study on the Instagram-Sharing Behaviors of Parents in the United Kingdom

Resourced From: SpringerLink / Children and Youth Services Review (CYYSR)

Writer / Contributor: Verswijvel, K., Walrave, M., Hardies, K., & Ponnet, K. (2019)

Overview: This study examined the motivations behind parental sharing behaviors on Instagram, revealing that many parents engage in "peer-induced sharenting" due to social comparison pressures. It found a significant relationship between peer influence and privacy violations, especially in mothers posting about younger children.

2. Title: The Impact of Sharenting

Resourced From: Taylor & Francis Online / Media International Australia

Writer / Contributor: Leaver, Tama & Highfield, Tim (2018)

Overview: This article presents sharenting as a spectrum, from casual photo sharing to full-fledged monetization and digital branding. It critiques platforms for capitalizing on child-centered content while offering little regulation.

3. Title: Sharenting: A Systematic Review of the Empirical Literature

Resourced From: Wiley Online Library / Journal of Family Theory & Review

Writer / Contributor: Tosuntaş, Ş. B. et al. (2024)

Overview: A comprehensive review of sharenting literature from multiple countries, organizing themes into motivations, risks, ethical issues, and children's autonomy. It also identifies gaps in digital literacy education for parents.

4. Title: Sharenting: Children's Privacy in the Age of Social Media

Resourced From: Emory Law Journal

Writer / Contributor: Steinberg, Stacey B. (2016)

Overview: Legal analysis of children's privacy rights in the digital age. It calls for new laws to govern parental digital consent and image ownership, especially where monetization is involved.

The Call to Action

Before You Post, Pause

This book is not about blame. It's about awareness. Not about stopping all sharing ~ but about shifting the *why*, the *how*, and the *for whom* behind every post.

We are the first generation of parents, carers, and educators to raise children in a digital world where privacy is no longer the default. Where photos live forever. Where innocent posts can ripple outward in ways we never imagined. And where our children grow up not just with memories ~ but with permanent records curated by others.

But we are also the first generation with the power to change that story.

Let's make a conscious decision, starting today.

✦ Ask before you post.

Even a five-year-old can be invited into a conversation about what feels okay. You're not just protecting privacy ~ you're building trust.

✦ Reflect on your motivation.

Is this memory for your family, or for your followers? Is this moment something your child will thank you for ~ or question you about?

✦ Set new norms in your circle.

Be the friend who checks before tagging. Be the relative who asks for consent. Be the educator who models digital respect.

✦ Advocate where it matters.

Support policy that protects children's digital rights. Speak up in schools, clubs, and online spaces. Digital dignity begins with a cultural shift.

✦ Share this message.

If this book made you pause, even once, it has done its work. But imagine what would happen if 10 more people paused too. And then 10 more.

This isn't about silence. It's about sovereignty. Your child's story is theirs. Your legacy is how you protected it.

So before you post... pause. Breathe. Ask. And choose with care.

Because the future is watching ~ and one day, it will ask who protected its voice.

#PauseBeforeYouPost

1. Not everything needs an audience.

2. They're your child, not your content.

3. A memory shared is a story rewritten.

4. Your love doesn't need likes.

5. The internet never forgets, but your child might want to.

6. One click today could echo for years.

7. Capture the moment ~ but don't capture their future.

8. Your child's privacy is worth more than your post.

9. Pause. Ask. Respect. Then decide.

10. Their story is still being written ~ don't edit it for them.

11. They didn't choose the spotlight ~ will you choose to protect them?

12. Before you post their smile, ask if it's yours to share.

13. A post for you ~ a footprint for them.

14. Protect now. Share later. Or maybe never.

15. What's cute today may feel exposed tomorrow.

www.ingramcontent.com/pod-product-compliance
Lightning Source LLC
Chambersburg PA
CBHW051658090426
42738CB00030B/3070